Difficult Riddles & Trivia Questions for Really Smart Kids: 100+ Brain Teasers that the Whole Family will Love

Jackie Bolen

Copyright © 2023 by Jackie Bolen

All rights reserved. No part of this publication may be reproduced, distributed, or transmitted in any form or by any means, including photocopying, recording or other electronic or mechanical means without the prior written permission of the publisher, except in the case of brief quotations in critical reviews and certain other non-commercial uses permitted by copyright law. For permission requests, write to the publisher/author at the following address: Jackie Bolen: jb.business.online@gmail.com.

Table of Contents

Difficult Riddles..4

Tough Riddles...7

Challenging Riddles..8

    Answers #1...9

Demanding Riddles...10

Onerous Riddles..11

Problematic Riddles..12

Strenuous Riddles...13

Bothersome Riddles..14

    Answers #2...15

Easier Said Than Done Riddles..16

Formidable Riddles...17

Herculean Riddles...18

Irritating Riddles...19

Toilsome Riddles..20

    Answers #3...21

Wearisome Riddles...22

Unyielding Riddles...23

Trying Riddles..24

Immense Riddles..25

Gargantuan Riddles..26

    Answers #4...27

Perplexing Trivia..28

Intricate Trivia..29

Involved Trivia...30

Uncompromising Trivia..31

Knotty Animal Trivia...32

    Answers #5...33

Ruthless Math Trivia..34

Colossal Geography Trivia...35

Tangled Geography Trivia..36

Impressive Trivia..37

Mighty Geography Trivia...38

    Answers #6...39

Lofty Body Trivia...40

Rigorous Language Trivia...41

Unrelenting Geography Trivia..42

Backbreaking Math Trivia..43

Taxing Language Trivia..44

    Answers #7...45

Punishing Body Trivia..46

Ultimate Holiday Trivia...47

Devastating Food Trivia...48

Only for Smart Kids Trivia...49

Too Difficult for your Parents Trivia?..50

    Answers #8...51

Difficult Riddles

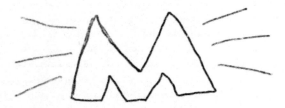

What is once in a minute, twice in a moment, but never in a thousand years?

Some people think I go too slow. Others think I go too fast. Most people are always checking me. What am I?

What is something that gets wetter as it dries?

See answers #1

Arduous Riddles

What can you catch, but not throw?

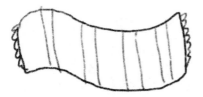

What is full of holes but can still hold water?

What food has no beginning, no middle and no end?

See answers #1

5

Ambitious Riddles

If you have one, you want to share it. If you share it, you haven't got it. What is it?

I have legs but I can't walk. A strong back but I don't do work. Two arms but I can't move them. What am I?

I have no lungs, but I can breathe. I have no life, but I live and die. I have no legs, but I can dance. What am I?

See answers #1

Tough Riddles

What goes up but never goes back down?

What goes down but never goes back up?

You have something that other people use far more often than you.

What is it?

See answers #1

Challenging Riddles

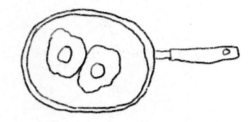

What do you have to break before you can use it?

What goes up when rain comes down?

What has a head, a foot, and four legs?

See answers #1

Answers #1

Difficult Riddles

- the letter M
- time
- towel

Arduous Riddles

- a cold
- sponge
- donut

Ambitious Riddles

- secret
- armchair
- fire

Tough Riddles

- age
- rain
- your name

Challenging Riddles

- egg
- umbrella
- bed

Demanding Riddles

If you cut me, I won't cry, but you will! What am I?

I have many eyes, but I cannot see. What am I?

I have more stories than any other building. What am I?

See answers #2

Onerous Riddles

I am a man, but I'll never have a wife. Water gives me life, but the sun brings death. What am I?

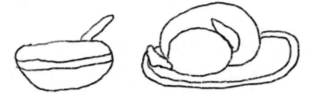

What are two things you can never eat for breakfast?

Tom was out for a walk. It started to rain, but he didn't have a jacket, hat, or umbrella. However, not a single hair on his head got wet. How?

See answers #2

Problematic Riddles

During which month do people sleep the least?

A man has six sons. Each son has a sister. How many children does the man have?

I start with a *P* and end with an *E* and have thousands of letters. What am I?

See answers #2

12

Strenuous Riddles

I can't speak, but I always tell the truth. What am I?

On a nice, sunny day a ship suddenly began to sink. There was nothing wrong with the ship. Why did it sink?

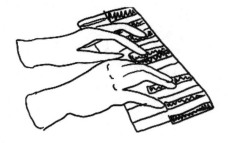

What has many keys, but can't open any doors?

See answers #2

Bothersome Riddles

What loses its head in the morning, but gets it back at night?

It has been around for millions of years, but it's never more than a month old. What is it?

How many seconds are there in a year? Hint-you don't need a calculator and the number is less than 100.

See answers #2

Answers #2

Demanding Riddles

- onion

- potato

- library

Onerous Riddles

- snowman

- lunch and dinner

- He's bald.

Problematic Riddles

- February—it has the fewest days.

- 7—6 boys and 1 girl

- post office

Strenuous Riddles

- mirror

- It's a submarine.

- piano

Bothersome Riddles

- pillow

- moon

- 24—each month has a 2nd and a 22nd.

Easier Said Than Done Riddles

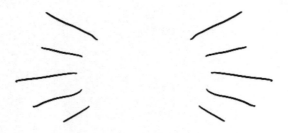

Dead people eat me all the time. Living people will die if they eat me. What am I?

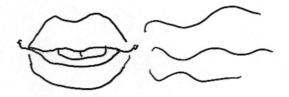

I'm in the air, but I'm not always there. I can be felt or held. It's easier to see me if you live in a cold place. What am I?

Who has married many people but has never been married?

See answers #3

Formidable Riddles

I am the most slippery country in the world. What am I?

I visit you every night but am lost every day. What am I?

I am the same from front to back and back to front, and you can drive me very fast. What am I?

See answers #3

Herculean Riddles

A 20-year-old man has had only five birthdays. How is that possible?

I can travel around the world without leaving the corner. What am I?

I never ask questions but am often answered. What am I?

See answers #3

Irritating Riddles

How can you add eight eights and get 1,000

You throw away the outside before you eat me and throw away the inside after you eat me. What am I?

Which is heavier—a ton of bricks or a ton of feathers?

See answers #3

Toilsome Riddles

I make a loud sound when I'm changing, and I get much bigger. What am I?

A bus driver was heading down the street. He went past three stop signs without stopping and was texting on his phone. The police saw him, but he didn't get in trouble. Why?

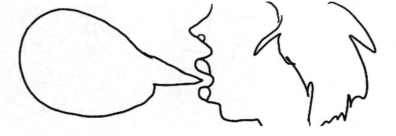

What goes away as soon as you talk about it?

See answers #3

Answers #3

Easier Said than Done Riddles

- nothing

- your breath

- priest

Formidable Riddles

- Greece—grease

- stars/moon

- race car

Herculean Riddles

- He was born on February 29th (leap year).

- stamp

- phone or doorbell

Irritating Riddles

- 888+88+8+8+8

- corn on the cob

- Neither—they both weigh a ton.

Toilsome Riddles

- popcorn

- He wasn't driving. He was walking.

- silence

Wearisome Riddles

I start and end with the letter E. I contain only one letter besides E. What am I?

How much dirt is there in a hole that is 3.45 m by 6.21 m? Hint: You don't need a calculator.

What has a face and two hands, but no arms and legs?

See answers #4

Unyielding Riddles

What is biggest when new but gets smaller with use?

I sometimes run, but I cannot walk. You always follow me around. What am I?

I am an odd number. Take away a letter and I become even. What number am I?

See answers #4

23

Trying Riddles

I am not alive, but I can die. What am I?

What has four fingers and a thumb but isn't living?

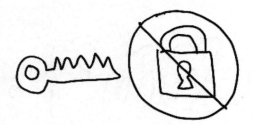

It has keys but no locks. It has space but no rooms. You can enter but can't go inside. What is it?

See answers #4

Immense Riddles

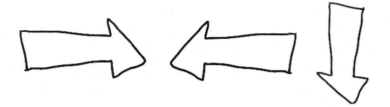

I am read the same forward, backward, and upside down. What am I?

The sun can bake them. Your hand can pick them. Your mouth can taste them. Your feet can walk on them. What are they?

This is an ancient invention still used today that allows people to see through walls.

See answers #4

Gargantuan Riddles

I am always coming, but I never arrive today. What am I?

A cat has one, a horse two, an elephant three. What am I?

Give me food and I grow. Give me water and I die. What am I?

See answers #4

Answers #4

Wearisome Riddles

- eye

- None because it's a hole.

- clock

Unyielding Riddles

- Many answers—soap, pencil, etc.

- your nose

- seven

Trying Riddles

- battery

- glove

- a keyboard

Immense Riddles

- swims, SOS

- grapes

- window or glass

Gargantuan Riddles

- tomorrow

- vowels (A, E, I, O, U)

- fire

Perplexing Trivia

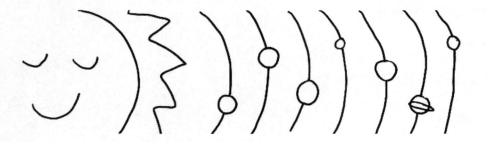

What is the hottest planet in our solar system?

Why can you see lightning before you can hear thunder?

Humans and animals need something in the air in order to live.

What is it?

See answers #5

Intricate Trivia

What is the deepest point in the ocean?

What gas, released by a car, stops your blood from carrying oxygen?

What do you call someone who studies plants?

See answers #5

Involved Trivia

What is a group of birds called?

What is the name of an adult female horse?

What are baby goats called?

See answers #5

Uncompromising Trivia

What is the study of birds called?

How many legs does a crab have?

How many toes does a dog have?

See answers #5

Knotty Animal Trivia

What kind of animal is a dolphin?

What is the largest primate in the world?

What is the deadliest snake in the world?

See answers #5

Answers #5

Perplexing Trivia

- Venus
- light
- Oxygen

Intricate Trivia

- Mariana Trench
- carbon monoxide
- botanist

Involved Trivia

- flock
- mare
- kids

Uncompromising Trivia

- Ornithology
- 10
- 18

Knotty Animal Trivia

- mammal
- Eastern gorilla
- black mamba

Ruthless Math Trivia

What do you call an object with six sides?

How many zeroes are in the number one hundred twenty-six thousand?

I bought three things at the store costing $1.44, $2.99, and $2.21. Tax is an extra 10%. How much will it cost?

See answers #6

Colossal Geography Trivia

What is the tallest mountain if you consider above and below the ocean? Hint: it's not Mount Everest or K2!

What is the world's largest lake?

What is the world's deepest lake?

See answers #6

Tangled Geography Trivia

Where does the leader of the Catholic Church, the Pope, live?

What is the capital of Northern Ireland?

What is the capital city of Australia?

See answers #6

Impressive Trivia

What is the second largest French-speaking city in the world?

What language do people speak in Brazil?

Korea is divided into North and South Korea. Which one is a friend of the USA?

See answers #6

Mighty Geography Trivia

What are the four maritime provinces of Canada?

Where does the Prime Minister of Britain live?

What is the only US state to have one syllable?

See answers #6

Answers #6

Ruthless Math Trivia

- hexagon

- 3

- $7.30

Colossal Geography Trivia

- Mauna Kea (more than ½ the height is underwater)

- Caspian Sea (Lake Superior is the largest freshwater lake)

- Lake Baikal

Tangled Geography Trivia

- Vatican City

- Belfast

- Canberra

Impressive Trivia

- Montreal, Canada

- Portuguese

- South Korea

Mighty Geography Trivia

- Newfoundland, New Brunswick, Nova Scotia, Prince Edward Island

- 10 Downing Street

- Maine

Lofty Body Trivia

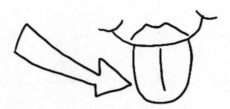

What are the things on your tongue that taste things?

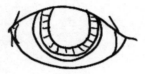

What is the colored part of the eye called?

What are the two holes in your nose called?

See answers #7

Rigorous Language Trivia

This person races horses for a job. What is the job name?

What document do you need if you want to travel to another country?

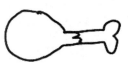

What is the name for a person or animal that eats both plants and meat?

See answers #7

Unrelenting Geography Trivia

What is the world's driest place?

What is the wettest place on Earth?

Where was the highest temperature on Earth recorded?

See answers #7

42

Backbreaking Math Trivia

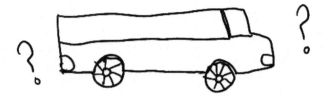

An empty bus pulls up to a stop, and 10 people get on. At the next stop, five people get off and twice as many people get on as at the first stop. At the third stop, 25 get off. How many people are on the bus?

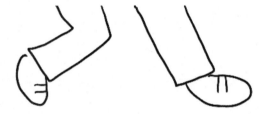

In gym class, Jen has to run around the track 15 times. Each lap is 400 m. How many kilometers does she run?

In kilometers, what is 10,500 meters?

See answers #7

Taxing Language Trivia

What is the job name for a person who studies rocks?

What does an entomologist study?

What is used to measure temperature?

See answers #7

Answers #7

Lofty Body Trivia

- taste buds

- the iris

- nostrils

Rigorous Language Trivia

- jockey

- passport

- omnivore

Unrelenting Geography Trivia

- Atacama Desert in Chile

- Mawsynram in India

- Death Valley, California

Backbreaking Math Trivia

- 1—the driver

- 6 kilometers

- 10.5 km

Taxing Language Trivia

- geologist

- insects

- thermometer

Punishing Body Trivia

How many bones does a human body have?

Where is the smallest bone in your body found?

What do antibiotics fight? What do they not fight?

See answers #8

Ultimate Holiday Trivia

What is the day after Christmas called in Canada, the UK, Ireland, Australia, and New Zealand?

During this holiday, you can't eat or drink from sunrise to sunset. What is it called?

What is the Korean thanksgiving festival called?

See answers #8

Devastating Food Trivia

What is the very large, smelly fruit that you can find in many Asian countries?

Which fruit was once known as a Chinese gooseberry?

Which fruit or vegetable has the highest fat content?

See answers #8

Only for Smart Kids Trivia

Which Disney princess is based on a real person?

What is the name of the Kung Fu Panda in the film with the same name?

Where can you catch the Hogwarts train?

See answers #8

Too Difficult for your Parents Trivia?

In golf, what is it called when you use one more shot than par? How about one less than par?

How many Olympic medals did American swimmer Michael Phelps win before he retired?

In snooker, what is the color of the last ball you have to sink?

See answers #8

Answers #8

Punishing Body Trivia

- 206

- Stapes/Stirrup (in the middle ear)

- bacteria, not viruses

Ultimate Holiday Trivia

- Boxing day

- Ramadan

- Chuseok

Devastating Food Trivia

- durian

- kiwi

- avocado

Only for Smart Kids Trivia

- Pocahontas

- Po

- Platform nine and three quarters at King's Cross Station

Too Difficult for Your Parent's Trivia?

- bogey, birdie

- 22

- black

Printed in Great Britain
by Amazon